Rock *YOUR* Red Carpet

Win Big on the Stage of Life

Rock *YOUR* Red Carpet

28 DAYS to ABUNDANCE

Michelle Moore Winder

Win Big on the Stage of Life

To Bill Winder
for allowing me to be me

You only have ONE Life to live. Live it well. You only have ONE Stage to shine on. Shine brightly. You only have ONE Red Carpet to Rock. ROCK IT like a ROCK STAR!

--- Michelle Winder

CONTENTS

Win Big on the Stage of Life

PROLOGUE

Confidence & Abundance

The most beautiful thing you can wear is confidence.

-- Blake Lively
American Actress

It's been said that the most beautiful thing a person can wear is confidence. As someone who's studied people for as long as I can remember, I would have to agree. Remember in junior high school, trying to figure out how the average guy got the gorgeous girl, and how the average girl got the hot guy. I realized by high school, it's all about confidence. It's like a magnet to people.

We have one life to live. We have one stage. We have limited time. I remember watching soap operas in college. I literally felt as though the actors were my friends. Pretty scary as I think about it now. I wasted hours of my life, sitting on the sofa my roommates found dumpster diving, watching other people live their purpose, not realizing I had the potential to live mine. It was almost 20 years later, after dying in the hospital, that I truly learned the *value* of time. In over 22 years of helping people all over the world, I've found that we often spend our time watching others, wishing *we* could do the amazing things *they* do or *be* the amazing people *they* are. All the while wasting our most precious limited resource- one we can't add to- our time.

Have you ever watched someone else's life and felt as though your own was flat in comparison? Have you given up on a dream because you felt you weren't beautiful enough, or young enough, or thin enough, or... just *enough?* You were designed with a plan and a purpose. A plan to give you hope and a future. Abundance is your birthright. Are you living it in every area of your life? Are you living an abundant life? Do you realize that *you,* my beautiful friend, have the ability to be the Rock Star on *your* stage of life?
Are you focusing on your *abundance* or on your *lack?* Are you living at full capacity, or is there room for improvement? Would you like to Lose Weight? Could you use more Money? Is there room to improve

your Intimate Relationships? Would you like to break a Habit? Feel more optimistic about your life? Be the best version of yourself? Do you feel like you've tried everything, without much success? Have you all but given up? If you've said yes to any of the above, then this challenge is for you. Not only will you become the best version of yourself in just 28 days, but you'll have the motivation you need to Rock YOUR Red Carpet. Take the challenge!

This challenge is based on the fact that there is One God, He designed you, He knows you personally, He loves you and His plan for you is good. His desire is that you would become the best version of you so you can fulfill the purpose He designed you for. He longs for you to experience

Abundance... possibly even more than *you* desire it for yourself.

Follow me step by step as your one-on-one personal trainer, mindset coach and experienced wealth coach. This Simple Step-by-Step guide will help you improve your life in areas including everything from physical health & fitness to true wealth in both your personal and professional lives.

The challenge is simple. Follow me closely for the next 28 days and I will prove it. You will learn to shine on your stage. By the end of the program, you will truly rock your red carpet. Then spread the word. You'll help others which is one of the most fulfilling things you can do.

I ask you to take this journey with me as I truly believe this challenge will greatly improve, if not completely change, your life. I don't ask this lightly. Although I am not religious in any way, I am a follower of Jesus and I live a life of love, joy, peace, power and miracles. I have yet to meet anyone, of any religion who, when confronted with the historical truth of the Man Jesus Christ of Nazareth, weren't moved by His overwhelming love, compassion and power. My personal story is compelling, and although I don't go into it here, I will tell you that my belief in God and His Son Jesus Christ is not by faith but by proof and by power. He has, literally, rescued me, healed me, and raised me from the dead. And I know for certain He will honor your sincere request to prove Himself.

Okay then, are you ready? Let's get started!

While this isn't mandatory, I suggest that you spend some time thinking about your goal before you write it. Sometimes, what we *think* we want isn't *really* what we want- it's, perhaps, a by-product or necessary component of something we really desire. It's important to take some time in your life to figure out your 'Why'- the very *root* of the reason you do what you do or why you want what you want. When you contemplate the deepest level of your *Why,* your desires may actually surprise you. Many people say their goal is to make a lot of money. But what are you willing to sacrifice to reach that goal? My purpose in writing this book, is so that people will realize that *time* is *life.*

Although it's easy to earn more money, we cannot add one moment to our life. We owe it to ourselves and to others, to optimize every minute. So think about this when you write your goal. Perhaps, deep down, you're not really willing to sacrifice your precious relationships, or a single moment of your valuable time, just to get rich. Spend some time on this important step. The next 28 days depend on you being honest with yourself. Take notes on pg. 156 - you'll use them again and again.

WRITE down your goal and tape it to your bathroom mirror or your computer screen. Someplace you will see it every day. Whether your goal is physical, like losing weight; transactional, like making more money, or emotional, such as having less anger or managing stress, be as specific as possible. And please be reasonable. You're not going to lose 100 pounds in 28 days- but you *can* lose 10 and change your life in the process. You may not become President of your company, but you may get that promotion you've been hoping for. Rather than making your goal to be a perfect spouse, how about fighting less? Make it something you can measure.

<u>NOTES</u>

WHOLEHEARTED THANKS

This book is dedicated to those of you who, without even trying, have encouraged and inspired me to write. Thank you for your constant willingness to listen to my views, however crazy they seemed at the time, and to make your position heard without discouraging me. I am truly thankful and dedicate this book to you:

To my #1 cheerleader & godly husband, Bill, I value your support more than I can put into words. To our beautiful children, Billy and Aubrey, your hearts for the struggling, your willingness to share your stories with me and your passion to help people who are hurting, motivated me to write this book.

Win Big on the Stage of Life

Removing Parasites from Spirit, Soul & Body

INTRO: PARASITES

Have you ever thought about Parasites?
Probably not. Do you have Parasites?
Probably. Most people do.
What is a Parasite?
Parasite

noun par·a·site \ˈper-ə-ˌsīt, ˈpa-rə-\

: an animal or plant that lives in or on another animal or plant and gets food or protection from it

: a person or thing that takes something from someone or something and does not do anything to earn it or deserve it

After reading this definition, think about this: Are *you* a Parasite? Yes, every single

21

one of us is. But there is a difference between positive parasites and negative. Were you ever in your mother's womb? Were you a nursing infant? We'll talk about undeserved grace later. What about the negative aspects?

Are you co-dependent? Are you living off others? Would you like to change into a self-sufficient, well-adjusted human being who is able to help others? If so, add it to your goal!

The interesting thing about Parasites is that often a person or animal has them with absolutely no signs, thus no idea they have them. By the time symptoms start showing up, the Parasites have multiplied and are literally sucking the life out of their victim. The longer you allow them to feed on you, the more severe and uncomfortable the symptoms become.

The victim becomes weaker and weaker and often doesn't understand why.

With that explanation, we're about to begin our 'cleanse.'

For some, this may be easy. For others, it will be one of the hardest things you've ever done. But it is simple I promise you, if you follow it carefully, step by step, you will be renewed, inside and out, in 28 days.

I suggest beginning on a Sunday, preferably the first of the month, as it's a new start and easier to map the days, but any day will do. Proper preparation will make it easier to navigate.

BEFORE you BEGIN:

1) Circle the first and last day of your cleanse on your Calendar. It can be paper or virtual, but mark those two days clearly. It is 28 days so 4- 7 day weeks.

2) WRITE your GOAL! Make it specific and measurable. Such as, "I will make an extra $5,000 per month."

3) If your goal is something like losing weight, decide how much (base it on safe measure, 2lbs/wk) So write, "I will lose 8 lbs. in 28 days. Then weigh yourself before you start and write it

down- don't weigh again until the 28 days are over.

4) Fill in the <u>blanks</u> on your sample week. You'll be using this as a template.

5) Adjust any times according to your personal schedule*

6) Print your shopping list** You can find everything you need at Costco, Trader Joes, Whole Foods or online.

7) SHOP (p.139)

8) Mix up your skincare recipes (p.131)

9) Make Special Fat Burning Water (p.131)

10) Put snack portions in baggies

If you can go without the snacks, it's better for your health. Make this a lifestyle, try to work toward dropping all snacks. When your body gets the nutrition it needs, you won't be hungry.

11) Prep Meals for the first 2-3 days

12) Set up Pandora with 'Kari Jobe' channel

13) Set up link for youtube.com on your phone or computer

14) Sign and Date the 28 Day Challenge Contract (p.29)

*While we understand that some people will need to adjust the times due to work schedules, etc. we suggest sticking as close to the schedule as possible as it's based on our created design. The way the menu is designed, it's easiest if you start on Sunday. I remember my sweet, loving, very successful grandpa always telling us, "Early to bed, early to rise, makes a man healthy, wealthy and wise." While I don't think he realized it was based on our bodily design & functions including hormones, I know he believed it as he experienced it first-hand!

Breakfast or lunch any day may be substituted with a fruit smoothie-
(recipe on pg. 131) I want to emphasize that fruit is good for you. Yes, even if

you're diabetic. There is so much misinformation going on out there. We can cure almost any disease with food. Our bodies were designed perfectly. If we give them the proper fuel and nutrition they require they serve us well.

Contact us for references.

Rock YOUR Red Carpet

28 DAY CHALLENGE CONTRACT

I, _____, hereby commit to closely follow the life-changing, *Coming Clean*, 28 Day Challenge. I will prepare, plan and follow through with each step outlined for the next 28 days. Although it may not always be easy, and I may not always understand how certain steps will help me, I look forward to the positive results of the cumulative steps, knowing that each step is designed for my benefit. I will not be bullied by my own insecurity or thoughts of failure. If I am tempted to cheat or skip steps, I will remember how much I value integrity. Looking forward to a "better me" in 28 days, I sign this contract with myself, of my own free will, and of a stable state of mind. No one is coercing me to make my whole life better. When I experience favorable results from this Challenge, I promise to share this method with, at least, two other people whom I believe will benefit from it.

I will Begin: _____ & End: _____

_____ / _____
Signature   Date

Win Big on the Stage of Life

WEEK 1

WEEK 1: Cleansing the Body

Remember the parasites from the Intro? Our bodies are bombarded by 'bad bugs' and toxins on a daily basis. While some people do drastic cleanses, it is this author's belief that our bodies are pretty good at taking care of themselves- IF we nourish and care for them properly. During this month, you should notice how eating 'real' food and getting small amounts of easy exercise will make you stronger, healthier and happier.

We have attached a 'sample week' here for you to follow throughout your 28 days. You may modify it, adjust the time, exercises and recipes to your liking- or you may toss it all together. However, we have found that *most* people don't realize that their eating habits, their words and their exercise plan (or lack thereof) have a HUGE influence on their mind, will and emotions.

Chances are, if you're reading this book, you need help with all of the above. In order to live a pain-free, joy-filled, life of freedom, we must address spirit, soul (mind, will, emotions) AND body. This 'sample week' makes it simple for you to follow. You can check out the shopping list to make adjustments.

We realize that most people have some sort of obligation during the day. Whether it be work, or care-giving, or school, or housekeeping, etc. You should find plenty of time within this schedule to do the things required of you. Otherwise, as said before, adjust the schedule to fit your needs.

*For those advanced students who would like to see changes more quickly, drop the bread and have your sandwiches as a salad.

Another excellent addition, as a fat burner and a lymph cleanser is to drink lemoniscious delight every morning first thing: Blend 2C water, ½ lemon, 1Tbs. virgin olive oil, 1 tsp vanilla. Strain & drink.

SAMPLE WEEK:
DAY 1 (Sunday)

"Whoever listens to Me will dwell safely and will be secure without fear" *Proverbs 1:33*

6am

> Wake Up. Say: "I'm thankful for a new day"
> Get Up. Rinse face and mouth with cool water.
> Oil Pull* with teaspoon of Coconut Oil 5-10 min
>
> Look in Mirror: Say: "You are Beautiful. You are Loved."
> Take Probiotic with 8 oz Special Water. 1-2 Cups Coffee/Tea

Watch:
www.youtube.com/watch?v=0yetHqWODp0

Walk for 5 minutes. Do 5 squats. Do 5 Counter Push-Ups.

Eat Breakfast: ½ grapefruit. Oatmeal with 1 tsp. coconut oil & ¼ c blueberries

Walk for 5 minutes.

Sip 16oz Water/lemon

Dry Brush your body, beginning with the feet, working upward toward the heart. Shower. Rinse with cold water for 10 seconds.

Listen to Pandora while grooming & dressing

8am

Say: "This is going to be a great day." 16 oz Water w/lemon. (Sip over an hour)

10am

1 cup hot tea w/tsp coconut oil. 8
Almonds. 3 dried Apricots.

12 noon

8 oz Water w/orange slice (sip over
hour- before lunch and after walk.
DO NOT drink with your meals)
Walk for 5 minutes
SAY: "I'm thankful for healthy food"
Sandwich: 2 slices Ezekiel sprouted
Bread, turkey, cheese, tomato,

lettuce, sprouts, cucumber, ½
avocado
SAY: "I will not be afraid of
_____" (insert your fear: failing,
what other people think, getting sick,
dying)

8 oz Water w/lemon. (sip over an hour)

3pm

8 oz special water. (Sip over an hour) 5 squats. Breathe in deeply through nose for 5 counts- Hold for 5 counts- Exhale through mouth 5 counts. (Be SURE to breathe from your diaphragm, NOT your chest. Your belly should extend beyond your chest when you inhale- not the other way around.
This is VERY important and will reduce stress just by breathing properly.)
Repeat Breathing Exercise 3 times. Best to do it outside in fresh air.
1 cup Ginger Tea w/tsp coconut oil. Handful of Pumpkin Seeds. Carrot

6pm

> Wash hands while saying: "I wash away painful memories and send them down the drain." (insert your weakness: Insecurity, etc)
> Look in Mirror: "You are confident. You are strong. You are Beautiful."
> DINNER: Greens Salad (Romaine, Spinach, Shredded Cabbage, celery, carrots, tomatoes, Greek Olives,
>
> Green Onions, cilantro) with ACV Dressing* topped with 8 oz Salmon
> 5 Dark Chocolate Almonds
> Walk 10 minutes (use a quick pace, no *strolling)*

*recipe pg. 131

8pm

> Walk 10 minutes.
> Say: "Even though my father
> _____(wasn't there for me,
> ignored me, insulted me, abandoned
> me, abused me) he loved me. I am
> loveable.
> I am valuable.
> Relax. Listen to Pandora.
> Cleanse face with Coconut Castor
> Whip* Wipe with warm washcloth.
> Rinse with warm water.
> WHITEN: Rub inside of Banana Peel
> over surface of teeth. Let sit 2 min.
> Brush teeth w/Xylitol Toothpaste.
> Spread light layer of Coconut whip
> over face and massage in.
> Blot w/tissue.

*recipe pg. 131

10pm

> Look in Mirror: "I'm thankful. Today was a good day. Tomorrow will be even better. You are Beautiful. You are valuable. You are loved. Sleep Well."
>
> Make sure room is cool (between 64-67 degrees is best for most people) and completely dark. Go to bed.

DAY 2

"For the Lord gives wisdom; from His mouth come knowledge and understanding." Proverbs 2:6

6am

> Wake Up. Say: "I'm thankful for a new day"
> Get Up. Rinse face and brush teeth with water.
> Look in Mirror: Say: "You are Beautiful. You are Loved."
> Take probiotic with 8 oz Special Water. 1-2 Cups Coffee/ tea.
> Watch:
> https://www.youtube.com/watch?v=0yetHqWODp0

Walk for 5 minutes. Do 5 squats. Do 5 Counter Push Ups.

Eat Oatmeal with 1 tsp. coconut oil & ¼ cup blueberries
Walk for 5 minutes. Sip 16oz Water/lemon
Brush teeth with Whitening Mixture*
Rub tsp coconut oil
on gums, swish, spit excess in Kleenex
Listen to Pandora while grooming & dressing.
*recipe pg. 131

8am

Say: "This is going to be a great day."
16 oz Water w/lemon. (Sip over an hour)

10am

> 1 cup hot tea w/tsp coconut oil. 8
> Almonds. 3 dried Apricots.

12 noon

> 8 oz Water w/orange slice
> SAY: "I'm thankful for healthy food"
> Sandwich: 2 slices Ezekiel Bread,
> turkey, cheese, tomato, lettuce,
> sprouts, cucumber, avocado
>
> SAY: "I will not be afraid of
> _____" (failing, what other
> people think, getting sick, dying)
> 8 oz Water w/lemon. (sip over an
> hour)

3pm

> 8 oz water. (Sip over an hour)

5 squats. Breathe in deeply through nose for 5 counts- Hold for 5 counts- Exhale through mouth 5 counts. Repeat Breathing Exercise 3 times.

1 cup Ginger Tea w/tsp coconut oil. Handful of Pumpkin Seeds. Carrot

6pm

Wash hands while saying: "I wash away painful memories and insecurity and send them down the drain."
Look in Mirror: "You are confident. You are strong. You are Beautiful."
DINNER: Greens Salad (Romaine, Spinach, Shredded Cabbage, celery, carrots, tomatoes, Greek Olives, Green Onions, cilantro) with ACV Dressing* topped with 8 oz Chicken

5 Dark Chocolate Almonds
Walk 10 minutes

8pm

Walk 10 minutes.
Say: "Even though my father
_____(ignored, insulted,
abandoned, abused) me, he loved
me. I am loveable. I am valuable.

Cleanse face with Coconut Castor
Whip* Wipe with warm washcloth.
Rinse with warm water.

Spread light layer of Coconut whip
over face and massage in.
Blot w/tissue.

MOVIE NIGHT
(choose from list on p.146)
Pan popped popcorn in Olive Oil
w/Sea Salt

10pm
Brush teeth w/Xylitol Toothpaste
then rub tsp coconut oil on gums spit
excess in Kleenex.
Look in Mirror: "I'm thankful. Today
was a good day. Tomorrow will be
even better.
You are Beautiful. You are valuable.
You are loved. Sleep Well."

DAY 3

"Do not be wise in your own eyes: Honor the Lord and depart from evil. It will be health to your flesh and strength to your bones."
Proverbs 3:7-8

6am

> Wake Up. Say: "I'm thankful for a new day"
> Get Up. Rinse face and mouth with cool water.
> Oil Pull* with teaspoon of Coconut Oil 10-15 min
> Look in Mirror: Say: "You are Beautiful. You are Loved."
> Take Probiotic w/8oz Special Water
> 1- 2 Cups Coffee /Tea.

Watch:
www.youtube.com/watch?v=v1C_qkjYllQ
Walk for 5 minutes. Do 5 squats, 5
Counter Push Ups.
Eat Breakfast: Oatmeal with 1 tsp.
coconut oil
& ¼ c blueberries
Walk for 5 minutes. Sip 16oz
Water/lemon
Shower- rinse with cold water
Listen to Pandora while grooming &
dressing

8am

Say: "This is going to be a great day."
16 oz Water w/lemon. (Sip over an
hour)

10am

1 cup hot tea w/tsp coconut oil. 8
Almonds. 3 dried Apricots.

12 noon

> 8 oz Water w/orange slice (sip over
> hour- before and after lunch.
> DO NOT drink during lunch)
> Walk for 5 minutes
> SAY: "I'm thankful for healthy food"
> Sandwich: 2 slices Ezekiel Bread,
> turkey, cheese, tomato, lettuce,
> sprouts, cucumber, avocado
> SAY: "I will not be afraid of
> _____" failing, what other
> people think, getting sick, dying
> 8 oz Water w/lemon. (sip over an
> hour)

3pm

> 8 oz water. (Sip over an hour)
> 5 squats. Breathe in deeply through
> nose for 5 counts- Hold 5 counts-

Exhale through mouth 5 counts.
Repeat Breathing Exercise 3 times.
Remember to use diaphragm
1 cup Ginger Tea w/tsp coconut oil.
Handful of Pumpkin Seeds.
½ Carrot

6pm

Wash hands while saying: "I wash
away painful memories and
insecurity and send them down the
drain."
Look in Mirror: "You are confident.
You are strong. You are Beautiful."
DINNER: Greens Salad (Romaine,
Spinach, Shredded Cabbage, celery,
carrots, tomatoes, Greek Olives,
Green Onions, cilantro) with ACV
Dressing* topped with 8 oz Salmon

DESSERT: 5 Dark Chocolate Almonds
Walk 10 minutes

8pm

Walk 10 minutes.
Say: "Even though my father
_____(wasn't there for me,
ignored me, insulted me, abandoned
me, abused me) he loved me.
I am loveable.
I am valuable.
Relax. Listen to Pandora.
Cleanse face with Coconut Castor
Whip* Wipe with warm washcloth.
Rinse with warm water.
WHITEN: Rub inside of Banana Peel
over surface of teeth.
Let sit 2 min. Brush teeth w/Xylitol
Toothpaste.

Spread light layer of Coconut whip
over face and massage in.
Blot w/tissue.

10pm

Look in Mirror: "I'm thankful. Today
was a good day. Tomorrow will be
even better.
You are Beautiful. You are valuable.
You are loved. Sleep Well."
Make sure room is cool and
completely dark. Go to bed.

DAY 4

"Keep My commands and live." Proverbs 4:4

6am

> Wake Up. Say: "I'm thankful for a new day"
> Get Up. Rinse face and mouth with cool water.
> Oil Pull* with teaspoon of Coconut Oil 10-15 min
> Look in Mirror: Say: "You are Beautiful. You are Loved."
> Take Probiotic w/ 8oz Special Water.
> 1-2 Cups Coffee /Tea.
> Watch:

www.youtube.com/watch?v=v1C_qkjYllQ

Walk for 5 minutes. Do 5 squats, 5 Counter Push Ups.

Eat Breakfast: Oatmeal with 1 tsp. coconut oil &

¼ c blueberries

Walk for 5 minutes. Sip 16oz Water/lemon

Listen to Pandora while grooming & dressing

8am

Say: "This is going to be a great day." 16 oz Water w/lemon. (Sip over an hour)

10am

1 cup hot tea w/tsp coconut oil. 8 Almonds. 3 dried Apricots.

12 noon

> 8 oz Water w/orange slice (sip over hour- before walk and after lunch. DO NOT drink during lunch)
> Walk for 5 minutes
> SAY: "I'm thankful for healthy food"
> Sandwich: 2 slices Ezekiel Bread, turkey, cheese, tomato, lettuce, sprouts, cucumber, avocado
> SAY: "I will not be afraid of
> _____" failing, what other people think, getting sick, dying
>
> 8 oz Water w/lemon. (sip over an hour)

3pm

> 8 oz water. Sip over an hour)

5 squats. Breathe in deeply through nose for 7 counts- Hold 7 counts- Exhale through mouth 7 counts. Repeat Breathing Exercise 3 times. 1 cup Ginger Tea w/tsp coconut oil. Handful of Pumpkin Seeds. Carrot

6pm

Wash hands while saying: "I wash away painful memories and insecurity and send them down the drain."
Look in Mirror: "You are confident. You are strong. You are Beautiful."
DINNER: Greens Salad (Romaine, Spinach, Arugula, Shredded Cabbage, celery, carrots, tomatoes, Greek Olives, Green Onions, cilantro) with ACV Dressing* topped with 8 oz chicken

5 Dark Chocolate Almonds
Walk 10 minutes

8pm

Walk 10 minutes.
Say: "Even though my father
_____(wasn't there for me,
ignored me, insulted me, abandoned
me, abused me) he loved me. I am
loveable.
I am valuable.
Relax. Listen to Pandora.
Cleanse face with Coconut Castor
Whip* Wipe with warm washcloth.
Rinse with warm water.

WHITEN: Rub inside of Banana Peel
over surface of teeth. Let sit 2 min.

Brush teeth w/Xylitol Toothpaste.

Spread light layer of Coconut whip
over face and massage in.
Blot w/tissue.

10pm

Look in Mirror: "I'm thankful. Today
was a good day. Tomorrow will be
even better.
You are Beautiful. You are valuable.
You are loved. Sleep Well."
Make sure room is cool and
completely dark. Go to bed.

DAY 5

"My words are life to those who find them, and health to all their flesh." Proverbs 4:22

6am

> Wake Up. Say: "I'm thankful for a new day"
> Get Up. Rinse face and mouth with cool water.
> Oil Pull* with teaspoon of Coconut Oil 10-15 min
> Look in Mirror: Say: "You are Beautiful. You are Loved."
> Take Probiotic w/ 8oz Special Water.
> 2 Cups Coffee/ Tea.
> Watch:

www.youtube.com/watch?v=v1C_qkjYllQ

> Walk for 5 minutes. Do 5 squats. Do 5 Counter Push Ups.

Eat Breakfast: ½ grapefruit. Oatmeal with 1 tsp. coconut oil & ¼ c blueberries
Walk for 5 minutes. Sip 16oz Water/lemon
Shower. Rinse with Cold water. Listen to Pandora while grooming & dressing

8am

Say: "This is going to be a great day." 16 oz Water w/lemon. (Sip over an hour)

10am

1 cup hot tea w/tsp coconut oil. 8 Almonds. 3 dried Figs.

12 noon

> 8 oz Water w/orange slice (sip over hour- before and after lunch.
> DO NOT drink during lunch)
> Walk for 5 minutes
> SAY: "I'm thankful for healthy food"
> Sandwich: 2 slices Ezekiel Bread, roast beef, cheese, tomato, lettuce, sprouts, cucumber, avocado
> SAY: "I will not be afraid of
> _____" failing, what other people think, getting sick, dying
> 8 oz Water w/lemon. (sip over an hour)

3pm

> 8 oz water. (Sip over an hour)
>
> 5 squats. Breathe in deeply through nose for 5 counts- Hold 5 counts- Exhale through mouth 5 counts.

Repeat Breathing Exercise 3 times.
1 cup Ginger Tea w/tsp coconut oil.
Handful of Pumpkin Seeds. Carrot

6pm

Wash hands while saying: "I wash
away painful memories and
insecurity send them down the
drain."
Look in Mirror: "You are confident.
You are strong. You are Beautiful."
DINNER: Greens Salad (Romaine,
Spinach, Arugula, Shredded Cabbage,
celery, carrots, tomatoes, Greek
Olives, Green Onions, cilantro) with
ACV Dressing* topped with 8 oz
chicken
DESSERT: 5 Dark Chocolate Almonds

8pm

Walk 10 minutes.

Say: "Even though my father
_____(wasn't there for me,
ignored me, insulted me, abandoned
me, abused me) he loved me. I am
loveable.

I am valuable.

Relax. Listen to Pandora.
Cleanse face with Coconut Castor
Whip* Wipe with warm washcloth.
Rinse with warm water.

WHITEN: Swish mouth with 3% food
grade hydogren peroxide 1 min.
Brush teeth w/Xylitol Toothpaste.
Spread light layer of Coconut whip
over face and massage in.

Blot w/tissue.

10pm

Look in Mirror: "I'm thankful. Today
was a good day. Tomorrow will be
even better.
You are Beautiful. You are valuable.
You are loved. Sleep Well."
Make sure room is cool and
completely dark. Go to bed.

DAY 6

"Teach us to number our days, that we may gain a heart of wisdom." Psalm 90:12

6am

Wake Up. Say: "I'm thankful for a new day"

Get Up. Rinse face and mouth with cool water.

Oil Pull* with teaspoon of Coconut Oil 10-15 min

Look in Mirror: Say: "You are Beautiful. You are Loved."

1-2 Cups Coffee or Tea.

Watch:

www.youtube.com/watch?v=v1C_qkjYllQ

Walk for 5 minutes. Do 5 squats. Do 5 Counter Push Ups.

Eat Breakfast: Oatmeal with 1 tsp. coconut oil & ¼ c blueberries
Walk for 5 minutes. Sip 16oz Water/lemon
Shower. Rinse with COLD water.
Listen to Pandora while grooming & dressing

8am

Say: "This is going to be a great day."
16 oz Water w/lemon. (Sip over an hour)

10am

1 cup hot tea w/tsp coconut oil. 8 Almonds. 3 dried Figs.

12 noon

8 oz Water w/orange slice (sip over hour- before and after lunch. DO NOT drink during lunch)
Walk for 5 minutes
SAY: "I'm thankful for healthy food"
Sandwich: 2 slices Ezekiel Bread, turkey, cheese, tomato, lettuce, sprouts, cucumber, avocado

SAY: "I will not be afraid of
_____" failing, what other people think, getting sick, dying
8 oz Water w/lemon. (sip over an hour)

3pm

8 oz water. (Sip over an hour)
5 squats. Breathe in deeply through nose for 5 counts- Hold 5 counts-

Exhale through mouth 5 counts.
Repeat Breathing Exercise 3 times.
1 cup Matcha Tea w/tsp coconut oil.
Handful of Pumpkin Seeds. Apple

6pm

Wash hands while saying: "I wash
away painful memories and
insecurity and send them down the
drain."
Look in Mirror: "You are confident.
You are strong. You are Beautiful."
DINNER: Greens Salad (Romaine,
Spinach, Shredded Cabbage, Arugula,
celery, carrots, tomatoes, Greek
Olives, Green Onions, cilantro) with

ACV Dressing* topped with 8 oz
Salmon
DESSERT: 5 Dark Chocolate Almonds

Walk 10 minutes

8pm

Walk 10 minutes.
Say: "Even though my father
_____(wasn't there for me,
ignored me, insulted me, abandoned
me, abused me) he loved me. I am
loveable.
I am valuable.

Relax. Listen to Pandora.
Cleanse face with Coconut Castor
Whip* Wipe with warm washcloth.

Rinse with warm water.
Work Coconut Castor Whip
throughout your hair. Cover in
plastic and cover w/towel.

WHITEN: Rub inside of Banana Peel over surface of teeth. Let sit 2 min.
Brush teeth w/Xylitol Toothpaste.
Spread light layer of Coconut whip over face and massage in.
Blot w/tissue.

10pm

Look in Mirror: "I'm thankful. Today was a good day. Tomorrow will be even better.
You are Beautiful. You are valuable.
You are loved.
Sleep Well."

Make sure room is cool (63-67 degrees) and completely dark. Go to bed.

DAY 7 (Saturday)

"Wisdom is length of days, riches, honor and peace." Proverbs 3:13-18

6-7am

Wake Up. Say: "I did it! I'm thankful for a good week! I'm a quarter of the way through my challenge!"

Get Up. Rinse face and mouth with cool water.

Look in Mirror: Say: "You are Beautiful. You are Loved."

Take Probiotic w/8oz Special Water.

1-2 Cups Coffee or Tea.

Watch:

www.youtube.com/watch?v=TJUh-Jeqfrg

Walk for 10 minutes. Do 5 squats, 5 Counter Push Ups, 5 jumping jacks

Shower. Rinse with cold water

Listen to Pandora while grooming & dressing

8am

Say: "This is going to be a great day."

16 oz Water w/lemon. (Sip over an hour)

10am

1 cup hot matcha tea w/tsp coconut oil.

Breakfast: 1 Hard boiled egg, Ezekiel toast, 1 Tbs. coconut oil, Tbs.jam

Walk for 5 minutes.

Sip 16oz Water/lemon

12 noon

    8 oz Water w/orange slice (sip over hour- before lunch and after walk. DO NOT drink during lunch)

    Walk for 5 minutes

    SAY: "I'm thankful for healthy food"

    Sandwich: 2 slices Ezekiel Bread, turkey, cheese, tomato, lettuce, sprouts, cucumber, avocado

    SAY: "I will not be afraid of _____" failing, what other people think, getting sick, dying

    8 oz Water w/lemon. (sip over an hour)

3pm

    8 oz water. (Sip over an hour)

    5 squats. Breathe in deeply through nose for 5 counts- Hold 5 counts- Exhale through mouth 5 counts.

Repeat Breathing Exercise 3 times.
1 cup Matcha Tea w/tsp coconut oil.
Favorite Muffin.

6pm

Wash hands while saying: "I wash
away painful memories & insecurity
and send them down the drain."
Look in Mirror: "You are confident.
You are strong. You are Healthy."
DINNER: Favorite Pizza, Greens Salad
w/ACV dressing, glass Red Wine
DESSERT: Vanilla yogurt
w/blueberries and 5 dark chocolate
almonds

8pm

Walk 15 minutes.

Say: "Even though my father
_____(wasn't there for me,
ignored me,
insulted me, abandoned me, abused
me) he loved me. I am loveable.
I am valuable.

Movie Night* (pg.) Pan popped
Popcorn w/Sea Salt
Cleanse face with Coconut Castor
Whip* Wipe with warm washcloth.
Rinse with warm water.

WHITEN: Rub inside of Banana Peel
over surface of teeth. Let sit 2 min.
Brush teeth w/Xylitol Toothpaste.

Spread light layer of Coconut whip
over face and massage in. Blot
w/tissue.

10pm

Look in Mirror: "You're AMAZING! You completed Week 1 of the Challenge! You're blessed. This week was a GREAT week. Next week will be even better! You are Beautiful. You are valuable. You are loved. Sleep Well." Make sure room is cool and completely dark. Go to bed.

Win Big on the Stage of Life

Financial Abundance

Before we head into Week 2, I'll share how you can add an additional $5k/mo to your income. After all, we're creating the 'abundant life' and we need money in order to help more people.
Once you get the hang of it, you can reproduce it over and over to add extra streams of income.

1) Choose a niche that you're passionate about and you have expertise in from these three money making niches:

   a) Health & Fitness: Weight loss, Nutrition, Diet, Coaching, Training
   b) Wealth: Make money online, affiliate marketing, e-commerce, Crypto Currencies
   c) Personal Development: Relationships, Parenting, Getting Back and Ex

2) Choose your Target Audience (a very specific avatar)
In this step, you want to actually picture a person: age, gender, marital status, income, habits, hobbies, reading materials, etc.- Get crystal clear on this for best effect.

3) Create an Amazon Best Seller E-Book
Write on a topic you're passionate about and expert in. If you're not expert, seek experts. Google has all the answers and info for life.

4) Make an Audio Book from the E-Book (you can use fiverr.com)

5) Set Up a Private Facebook Group

6) Package the e-book, audio book & Private FB Group together

7) Market to your Avatar (using Social Media and email Marketing)

Once you have this down, you can set up a sales funnel and look forward to streaming income, 7/24. Become an expert in a related topic, or something else you're passionate about and add an additional stream of income.

NOTES

WEEK 2

WEEK 2 - Cleansing the Soul

What is your soul? It's *probably* not what you think! *Most* people are confused by the term 'soul' so I will give the definition here.

Soul

noun \'sōl\

the immaterial essence, principle, or actuating cause of an individual life

the moral and emotional nature of human beings

In other words, our soul is our mind, our will and our emotions.

This is what separates us from the animal world.

This week, we want to focus on changing our thinking. Recent Scientific evidence now proves that what we think has a direct effect on our physical body. Our brains actually rewire according to our thoughts. Funny, God told us that in the Bible over 2000 years ago. Do you know that our brains can't actually distinguish between reality and fiction? What are you watching on TV & Movies? Your brain believes it's real. So, let's change our stinkin' thinkin! Think positive! Watch positive, encouraging movies.

Remember the old proverb: Trash In, Trash Out.

One of the reasons I love working with people to change their thinking is because studies show that 97% of people die with regrets! That is unacceptable to me. Especially, when it's so simple to take control of your life so that you can live your purpose and go in peace when it's time.

On another note, many people struggle with confidence, a key component in making your dreams come true. Have you ever heard the old saying, "fake it till you make it?" I've taught self defense and personal safety for over 20 years and one thing I always teach: If you are insecure or shy, do *not* show it! Predators can spot a victim from a mile away. Pretend you are confident and others will react likewise. Try this for 3 days and you will notice a difference in your attitude. Walk tall with shoulders back. Make eye contact with strangers as you walk by. Smile at people this week. You'll find people are nicer and friendlier than you thought! Added bonus: you'll look younger! Without exception, everyone I've talked to who's tried this told me it completely changed their outlook. They never realized people could be so nice and friendly. Consider this: how much of what we get is directly related to what we're putting out there? Life is short, be nice!

Wear well tailored clothes and walk with your head up and shoulders back and you will look younger, smarter, and more attractive. Confidence is a magnet.

Days 8 through 14 follow the approximate template from the Sample week. Remember, you can substitute meals but don't stray too far...use the shopping list and stay within the guidelines. In addition, read the quotes for each day multiple times throughout the day. Remember, words matter. Say them out loud and change your thinking.

Win Big on the Stage of Life

DAY 8 (Sunday)

"Cast your cares on the Lord and He will sustain you." Psalm 55:22
"Cast all your cares (anxiety) on Him, for He cares for you." 1Peter 5:7

DAY 9 (Monday)

"Whoever dwells in the shelter of the Most High will rest in the shadow of the Almighty" Psalm 91:1

DAY 10 (Tuesday)

"I will walk in freedom for I seek Your precepts." Psalm 119:45

DAY 11(Wednesday)

"For the Lord is good; His mercy is everlasting." Psalm 100:5

DAY 12 (Thursday)
"And my God shall supply all your needs according to His riches in glory by Christ Jesus." Philippians 4:19

DAY 13 (Friday)
"For I will restore health to you and heal you of your wounds,' says the Lord" Jeremiah 30:17

DAY 14 (Saturday)
"Bless the LORD, O my soul, and forget not all His benefits: Who forgives all your iniquities, Who heals all your diseases." Psalms 103:2-3

Now that you're half way through the challenge, re-assess every area of your life. Don't be hard on yourself if the changes aren't huge- it's only been two weeks, but you should definitely notice changes. How do you feel? How has your outlook changed? How about your energy? Are you sleeping better? What have you learned? How are others responding to you?
Have you worked on your e-book? Write down some noticeable changes and celebrate your good work! You are a champion and you can do this!

NOTES

FAST FIT

Before we head into week 3, and focus on our inner being, this is a perfect time to add a little insert here to 'uplevel' our outer being. This 5 minute add-on is a game-changer! Add this before breakfast, and skip
the exercises in the Sample Week. It may seem slightly hard at first, but keep it up! It gets easier every day! Check it out:

COMBAT BODY WORKOUT

- Want to lose 5 pounds in just 5 minutes in 5 days and get in the best shape of your life?
- Would you like a simple, practical workout that the military in many countries has used for ages?
- No complicated moves. No time-consuming programs. No expensive workout equipment. No gym membership.

Welcome to Combat Body! Your full-body, go-anywhere workout that's both simple and effective and it doesn't take up space or your valuable time.
Are you ready to Rock YOUR Red Carpet?

LOSE 5 LBS in 5 MIN in 5 DAYS
Rest 10 seconds between each exercise

1. **Jumping Jacks 45 sec countdown**
   Start with arms by your sides
   Jump up, feet apart, touch hands
   over head
   Back to start and repeat

2. **Push-Ups 30 second countdown**
   Hands shoulder width apart
   Back Straight, legs straight* elbows
   close to body
   Lower chest to ground & rise back up
   *you can start on your knees until you get
   stronger

3. **Squats 60 sec countdown**
   Feet shoulder width apart

Squat down till thighs are parallel with floor

Keep back straight and toes pointing forward

4. **Lunges 30 sec countdown** Feet shoulder width apart, hands on hips

Step out with Right leg, lowering left knee to floor

Back to start, repeat with left knee, alternating

5. **Mountain Climbers 15 sec countdown**

Start in push-up position

Bring right knee into chest, then back to start

Repeat with left knee, alternating

6. Reverse Lunges 30 sec countdown

Feet shoulder width apart, hands on hips

Step back with Right leg, lowering left knee to floor

Back to start, repeat with left leg, alternating

7. Jumping Jacks 30 sec countdown

To accelerate fat loss, drink Lemoniscious first thing in the morning, then do your workout, before eating or drinking anything else. Come on, it's only 5 minutes! You'll have extra energy for the day!

*Lemonisciuos Recipe:
- 2 C pure water
- 1 whole lemon (cut in half)
- 1 Tbs Olive Oil
- 1 tsp vanilla

Blend well. Strain. Drink

Rock YOUR Red Carpet

Disclaimer: Please review the following User Agreement carefully before attempting this or any exercise program. We strongly recommend that you consult with your physician before beginning any exercise program. You should be in good physical condition and be able to participate in the exercise. Michelle Winder and RockYOURRedCarpet.com is not a licensed medical care provider and represents that it has no expertise in diagnosing, examining, or treating medical conditions of any kind, or in determining the effect of any specific exercise on a medical condition. You should understand that when participating in any exercise or exercise program, there is the possibility of physical injury. If you engage in this exercise or exercise program, you agree that you do so at your own risk, are voluntarily participating in these activities, assume all risk of injury to yourself, and agree to release and discharge RockYOURRedCarpet.com & Michelle Winder from any and all claims or causes of action, known or unknown, arising out of this Combat Body Workout or negligence.

Win Big on the Stage of Life

WEEK 3

Days 15 through 21 follow the approximate template from the Sample week. Remember, you can substitute meals but don't stray too far... stay within the guidelines. In addition, read the quotes for each day multiple times throughout the day. Remember, words matter. Say the quotes out loud, try to memorize the ones that stand out to you and change your thinking.

WEEK 3- REVIVING THE SPIRIT

GREAT Job! You're half way there! Focus on how great you feel!

Spirit

*1: an animating or vital principle held to **give life** to physical beings*
*2: the principle of conscious life; the **vital principle** in humans, animating the body and mediating between body and soul.*
*3: A **supernatural being or essence**: such as the HOLY SPIRIT*

Our world is a mess. You don't have to watch more than 5 minutes of the news to know it. Look at our government. Look at the lives around you. Look at your own life. Are you experiencing love, joy and peace on a daily basis?

Our generation, especially in the US, has desperately tried to separate spirit, soul, and body. Remember from last week, our soul is our mind, will and emotions? According to the definition above, our spirit is what mediates between our body and our mind, will and emotions. Many people don't even realize they *have* a spirit. So what happens when the body tells the mind what to do, or the mind tells the body what to do, ignoring the spirit-whose job it is? Look around, you'll see it clearly. We're living in times of selfishness and confusion and I believe it's due to this missing link. The fact remains that we are all three at once, body, soul and spirit. It's what makes us *human*. It is impossible to separate us.

We often run from God or ignore Him all together. But when we try to hide from our Creator, we're only fooling our minds and bodies in the process. Our spirit knows the truth. We try to run our lives at 2/3 efficiency- max. In turn, we create confusion, sickness and even death in our lives. Death of dreams, death of relationships, death of purpose... need I go on?

BUT, there's good news! We have a Good Good Father in Heaven:

The high and lofty one who lives in eternity, the Holy One, says this: "I live in the high and holy place with those whose spirits are contrite and humble. I restore the crushed

spirit of the humble and revive the courage of those with repentant hearts.
Isaiah 57:15

What are you feeding your spirit? The *truth* of God's word? Or the *foolishness* of man's wisdom?

One of the coolest things about God, in my opinion, is that His power and love aren't limited by one's belief or lack thereof! He's still powerful and He still loves you, even if you don't believe He exists. THAT is unconditional, relentless, radical love!

DAY 15 (Sunday)
The wages of sin is death, but the gift of God is eternal life in Christ Jesus our Lord. Romans 6:23

DAY 16 (Monday)
If any of you lacks wisdom, let him ask of God, who gives to all liberally and without reproach, and it will be given to him. James 1:5

DAY 17 (Tuesday)
Trust in the Lord with all your heart, And lean not on your own understanding; In all your ways acknowledge Him, And He shall direct your paths. Proverbs 3:5-6

DAY 18 (Wednesday)
Bless the LORD, O my soul, And forget not all His benefits: Who forgives all your iniquities, Who heals all your diseases.

Psalms 103:2-3

DAY 19 (Thursday)
"Bless the LORD, O my soul, And forget not all His benefits: Who forgives all your iniquities, Who heals all your diseases."
Psalms 103:2-3

DAY 20 (Friday)
"I will give you a new heart and put a new spirit within you; I will take the heart of stone out of your flesh and give you a heart of flesh." Ezekiel 36:26

DAY 21 (Saturday)
If we confess our sins, He is faithful and just to forgive us our sins and to cleanse us from all unrighteousness. 1 John 1:9

Rock YOUR Red Carpet

WEEK 4

Days 22 through 28 follow the approximate template from the Sample week. Remember, you can substitute meals but don't stray too far... stay within the guidelines. In addition, read the quotes for each day multiple times throughout the day. Remember, words matter. Say them out loud and change your thinking.

Win Big on the Stage of Life

WEEK 4 - Coming Clean

Therefore, since we are surrounded by such a huge crowd of witnesses to the life of faith, let us strip off every weight that slows us down, especially the sin that so easily trips us up. And let us run with endurance the race God has set before us. Hebrews 12:1 NLT

You're in the home stretch. Keep your eyes on the finish line. You've done an amazing job and you're almost done! Write down your thoughts about how you feel.

Reassess where you were and how far you've come. Celebrate even small changes. Realize that you can accomplish anything you set your mind to. You're amazing!

For an added boost, make an appointment for a new hairstyle or highlights or a free makeover at the Mac counter. Buy a new pair of shoes or a new blouse or dress, or a new shirt, tie, or accessory. Take a trusted friend shopping and try out new colors. Try a new style! Have fun and pay attention to how you feel.

Take a nature walk or hike and pay attention to the birds and the fresh air. Breathe deeply. Get 15 minutes of sun every day on as much of your body as possible. Try not to wear sunglasses when possible. Remember, Vitamin D from the sun is actually a hormone that regulates all of your cells. It's the best cancer inhibitor known to man. If you use sunscreen, make sure it's all natural; literally safe to eat.

Your skin is your largest organ and it drinks in everything that you put on it. Beware of toxins.

Keep Your Eyes on the Goal

To say our daughter loves horses would be an understatement. She's been called 'the horse whisperer' since she was 14 years old, while calming a huge black stallion who was being rescued from the San Diego fires in 2007. She now works with Race Horses so it's really fun to go to the races with her because she *knows* horses. She exercises them in the morning before they run so she knows their mood, their individual personalities, temperaments and habits. I'll never forget one time we went to Del Mar on a specific day to see her favorite horse run. She loved this little gray filly and told us she would win. We rarely bet but Aubrey was so insistent we decided to place a bet.

As the horses thundered out of the starting gate, her little cutie was in last place! Dead last! I was surprised because our daughter was usually right on. Then, as the horses approached the last turn, Aubrey said, "Now watch her closely." This little filly was 2 lengths behind the last horse. I knew there was no hope. Suddenly, this little girl picked up speed, she caught up. She passed a few horses and we were thrilled that she wouldn't be in last place. We had already committed to losing our five bucks. But as we watched, she rounded from the outside lane and overtook horse by horse until she was nose to nose with the horse in 2nd place on the home stretch. Everyone was on their feet. There was screaming and shouting as this little gray filly passed the 2nd place horse... passed the horse in the lead and won the race by 4 lengths!

I'll *never* forget that day. She was so relaxed at the starting gate. To most of us watching, she seemed way too slow to finish well. I learned a very valuable lesson that day. It doesn't matter if you start off slowly, or even poorly. What matters is what happens in the home stretch.
Keep your eyes on the finish line! You're about to win in the race of life.

DAY 22 (Sunday)
"Be anxious for nothing, but in everything by prayer and supplication with thanksgiving let your requests be made known to God."
Philippians 4:6

DAY 23 (Monday)
"I sought the Lord, and He heard me, and delivered me from all my fears." Psalm 34:4

DAY 24 (Tuesday)
"Peace I leave with you, My peace I give to you; not as the world gives do I give to you. Let not your heart be troubled, neither let it be afraid." John 14:27

DAY 25 (Wednesday)
"There is no fear in love; but perfect love casts out fear, because fear involves torment."
1 John 4:18

DAY 26 (Thursday)
"But He said, "The things which are impossible with men are possible with God." Luke 18:27

DAY 27 (Friday)
"For all the promises of God are Yes and Amen in Jesus"
2 Corinthians 1:20
"And this is the promise that He has promised us—eternal life."
1 John 2:25

DAY 28 (Saturday)

"Having been justified by faith we have peace with God through our Lord Jesus Christ." Romans 5:1

CONGRATULATIONS!!

You have finished the 28 Day Challenge! Grab your Contract and your Goal Sheet. Sign off on them. You have obtained your goal! How are you feeling? Are you ready to make this a lifestyle? You are more than a conqueror! You can do anything you set your mind to. With God, ALL THINGS are POSSIBLE! You can change the world! Run with endurance and keep your eyes on the finish line!

Our suggestion is that you repeat the steps in this workbook 3 times. (90 days.) Put on your best outfit that makes you feel confident! You are now ready to Rock YOUR Red Carpet and win BIG on your stage of life! If you would like help getting publicity for your passion, and would like to physically walk the Red Carpet, photos and all, please contact us through our website at: www.RockYourRedCarpet.com Let us know that you have finished the book and are ready to ROCK! We'll send you an email, asking you to send before and after pics and a short (30-60 second) testimonial. We'll then send you information on how you can proceed in getting publicity as well as photos on a real red carpet!

All Scripture, unless otherwise noted, is from the New King James Version

SCRIPTURE:

For I know the thoughts that I think toward you, says the Lord, thoughts of peace and not of evil, to give you a future and a hope.
- **Jeremiah 29:11**

Give all your worries and cares to God, for He cares about you. —
1 Peter 5:7, NLT

The fear of man brings a snare, but whoever trusts in the Lord shall be safe. -
Proverbs 29:25

Fear not, for I am with you; be not dismayed, for I am your God. I will strengthen you, yes, I will help you, I will uphold you with My righteous right hand. -
Isaiah 41:10

For God has not given us a spirit of fear, but of power and of love and of a sound mind.
2 Timothy 1:7

For all the promises of God are Yes and Amen in Him, to the glory of God through us.
2 Corinthians 1:20

As for God, His way is perfect; the word of the Lord is proven; He is a shield to all who trust in Him.
Psalm 18:30

For sin shall not have dominion over you, for you are not under law but under grace.
Romans 6:14

"...I am the Lord who heals you." —
Exodus 15:26

When the sun was setting, all those who had any that were sick with various diseases brought them to Him; and He laid His hands on every one of them and healed them all. — **Luke 4:40**

The Lord will command the blessing on you in your storehouses and in all to which you set your hand, and He will bless you in the land which the Lord your God is giving you.
Deuteronomy 28:8

Delight yourself in the Lord, and He shall give you the desires of your heart. —
Psalm 37:4

Call to Me, and I will answer you, and show you great and mighty things, which you do not know.
Jeremiah 33:3

Jesus replied, "I am the bread of life. Whoever comes to me will never be hungry again. Whoever believes in me will never be thirsty. — **John 6:35, NLT**

Now to Him who is able to do exceedingly abundantly above all that we ask or think, according to the power that works in us.
Ephesians 3:20

The faithful love of the Lord never ends! His mercies never cease. Great is his faithfulness; His mercies begin afresh each morning. **Lamentations 3:22–23, NLT**

These things I have spoken to you, that in Me you may have peace. In the world you have tribulation; but be of good cheer, I have overcome the world. **- John 16:33**

PRAYERS:

Prayer for Salvation:

"Dear God, I know I'm a sinner, and I ask for your forgiveness. I believe Jesus Christ is Your Son. I believe that He died for my sins and that you raised Him to life. I want to trust Him as my Savior and follow Him as Lord, from this day forward. Guide my life and help me to do your will. I pray this in the name of Jesus. Amen."

Prayer For Healing:

"Lord Jesus, I thank You that You love me and that You are both able and willing to heal me. At the cross, You took all my sicknesses and pain in Your own body, and by Your stripes, I am healed! Your body was scourged and broken so that mine can be whole. I receive all that You have done for me and I rest in Your finished work. There is nothing more for me to do. As I wait on You for the complete manifestation of my healing, I choose to focus on and give praise for Your great love for me. Amen!" (www.JosephPrince.org)

Pray:
https://www.youtube.com/watch?v=luVsY96vAfw
Provision:
https://www.youtube.com/watch?v=743M2kIqH6s
Jesus:
https://www.youtube.com/watch?v=2JQoC0JwHlg
Rest & Receive at Jesus' Feet:
https://www.youtube.com/watch?v=bJagBsXabi4
Rest in Jesus for Healing:
https://www.youtube.com/watch?v=JfRGkm47N5c
Hope:
https://www.youtube.com/watch?v=pcEZJ8yUPXg

RECIPES:

FRUIT SMOOTHIE*

1 C. Full Fat Greek Yogurt (plain or vanilla)

2 Scoops Vanilla Protein Powder

½ C Matcha/Ginger Tea (cold)

½ C Coconut Milk (not water)

1 whole orange

tsp. fresh ginger & turmeric

1 Frozen Banana

tsp. flax, chia, hemp seed

1 C Frozen Pineapple

2 raw organic eggs

- shredded coconut optional

Blend in good blender such as VitaMix or Ninja or Blendtec...add ice as needed

*(may be used to replace any breakfast or lunch)

SPECIAL FAT BURNING WATER:

Fill ½ gallo
n glass pitcher with good water
Add sliced cucumber, lime, fresh cilantro
Add Grated Ginger and Grated Turmeric
 Let sit over night

ACV SALAD DRESSING

¾ C Apple Cider Vinegar (Organic Unfiltered) TJ's is great!

¼ C balsamic Vinegar

2 C Virgin Olive Oil

1 tsp. Garlic Salt

1 tsp. Onion Powder

1 Tsp. Tuscan Style Italian Seasonings

TEETH WHITENING:

1) Slice off bottom 1/3 of banana peel.

2) Scrub teeth with inside of peel

3) Let sit on teeth 2 min.

4) Rinse thoroughly

OIL CLEANSING METHOD:

1. Massage a small amount of the Whipped Facial Cleanser* gently into your face and neck.

2. Allow the oils to penetrate into the skin.

3. Soak a soft wash cloth in hot water, ring out, press over face to steam

4. Wipe clean with washcloth, repeat steam process.

*WHIPPED FACIAL CLEANSER

1 C Coconut Oil

1/2 C Castor Oil

3 Drops Frankincense EO

Whip Coconut Oil until light and fluffy.

Drizzle in Castor Oil and EO and continue whipping.

When blended, store in air tight container.

KIDNEY CLEANSE

1/3 C Knudsen Black Cherry juice

1/2 C Santa Cruz Organic Apple juice

2 TBS Lemon Juice (fresh squeezed)

This is an amazing Kidney Cleanse- and delicious! Lemon juice dissolves kidney stones. Black cherry juice flushes uric acid...also helpful for arthritis. I serve this at parties and it's the first drink to go!

Win Big on the Stage of Life

SHOP

Shop

Before we get to the Shopping List, we'd like to say that what you don't eat is as important as what you do. Immediately throw out ALL FAKE SUGAR, ALL DIET FOODS. Besides being terrible for your blood sugar, body and mind, they're making you FAT! Throw out ALL TOOTHPASTE containing FLOURIDE, which is toxic AND contains either aspartame (making you fat) or sugar, giving you cavities! Marketing can be very deceptive. Other examples are all the hidden neurotoxins such as MSG & aspartame, marketed under names like 'vanillin' (hidden in most chocolate) and "other spices." Stevia, on the other hand, in its pure liquid form is actually good for you and cleanses the pancreas, but companies have processed it to a white powder which is sweet but not beneficial, yet some, to a point where it can be harmful. There's a huge difference. Do NOT eat anything soy related. It is NOT good for you. Limit corn to movie night popcorn. It's a grain, NOT a vegetable, and it's all genetically modified and not good for you. If you have questions, please contact us.

SHOPPING LIST

Hydrogen Peroxide (food grade is best but MUST be diluted to 3%)
High Quality Probiotics
Raw Unfiltered Honey

Xylitol Toothpaste (NOW Xyli-White)
Frankincense EO
Vanilla Protein Powder (High Quality NO SOY!)
Extra Virgin Olive Oil

Organic Cold Pressed Coconut Oil
Castor Oil
Avocado Oil

Good Earth Matcha Maker Tea
Ginger Tea
Coconut Milk
Raw Unfiltered Apple Cider Vinegar
Greek Olives

Dried Apricots
Dried Figs
Almonds
Brazil Nuts
Pumpkin Seeds
Sunflower Seeds

Cilantro
Mint
Ginger Root
Turmeric Root

Cucumber
Celery
Carrots
Spinach
Romaine
Arugula
Tomatoes   (unless your AB blood type)
Sprouts
Red or Yellow Bell Peppers

Sweet Potatoes
Bananas
Lemons
Limes
Oranges
Pink Grapefruit
Pears
Green Apples
Red Apples
Blueberries, Raspberries, Strawberries (fresh or frozen)
Frozen Pineapple

Greek Yogurt (full fat) Plain or Vanilla
Whole Oats
Ezekiel Sprouted Bread

Eggs- Organic farm raised**
Organic Turkey Breast
Organic Grain Fed Ground Beef
Wild Caught Salmon (canned is fine)

Dark Chocolate Almonds with Sea Salt

*This is a standard shopping list. We realize people have different dietary needs so adjust accordingly. Feel free to substitute if you are Gluten Free, Paleo, Vegan or Vegetarian. HOWEVER, try to follow the menus as closely as possible. If you need help with alternatives, contact us. Please **do not**, under any circumstance, replace whole foods with processed fake foods.

**If you can only afford to buy ONE thing Organic make it your EGGS! You can probably find them raised locally on Craigslist cheaper than regular eggs at the grocery store.

MOVIES

INSPIRATIONAL MOVIES:

1. A Beautiful Mind
2. The Pursuit of Happyness
3. The Blind Side
4. Fireproof
5. Grace Unplugged
6. Erin Brockovich
7. Lord of the Rings
8. Remember the Titans
9. Chariots of Fire
10. Billy Elliot
11. We are Marshall
12. Rudy
13. Finding Nemo
14. Eternal Sunshine of the Spotless Mind
15. In America

COMEDY:
1. What About Bob?
2. Pitch Perfect
3. Two Weeks Notice
4. Meet The Parents
5. The Proposal
6. 100 First Dates
7. Roxanne
8. Beverly Hills Cop
9. Miss Congeniality
10. Father of the Bride

Rock YOUR Red Carpet

<u>NOTES</u>

<u>NOTES</u>

<u>NOTES</u>

<u>NOTES</u>

<u>NOTES</u>

About the Author

Michelle's passion is to help people recognize *time* as *life.* While working with victims and teaching self defense for over 22 years, Michelle realized that too many of us are *watching others* while our own valuable life slips by. In 2017, she founded Rock *YOUR* Red Carpet, showing people how to live their passion, so they can rock their own red carpet. Michelle & her husband, Bill, live in San Diego, CA. They also own a horse & cattle ranch on the outskirts of Lexington, Kentucky. Their children are married and their first grandson is on the way.

Other Books By The Author
Disruptive Life Strategy:
28 Days to Confidence & Success
Dark Road Home

CONTACT the AUTHOR

To contact Michelle Winder for information or for invitations for speaking engagements:

Email: 1sup@att.net
Website: www.RockYourRedCarpet.com

Rock YOUR Red Carpet

Made in the USA
Las Vegas, NV
11 November 2021

34080798R00089